SLOUCHING TOWARD RADIANCE

Slouching
toward Radiance

A Day in the Life of You, Me, and God

Heidi Barr

with art by Emily Anderson

WAYFARER BOOKS
BERKSHIRE MOUNTAINS, MASSACHUSETTS

WAYFARER BOOKS

WAYFARERBOOK.ORG

Quantity sales. Special discounts are available on quantity purchases
by corporations, associations, bookstores, and others. For details, contact the
publisher or visit wholesalers such as Ingram or Baker & Taylor.

All Rights Reserved
Published in 2022 by Wayfarer Books
Cover Design and Interior Design by Leslie M. Browning
Cover Image: Emily Anderson
ISBN: 978-1953340504
First Edition Trade Paperback

10 9 8 7 6 5 4 3 2 1

Look for our titles in paperback, ebook, and audiobook wherever books are sold.
Wholesale offerings for retailers available through Ingram.

Wayfarer Books is committed to ecological stewardship.
We greatly value the natural environment and invest in
environmental conservation. For each book purchased in our
online store we plant one tree.

For Nick

The dance of renewal, the dance that made the world,
was always danced here at the edge of things.

—Ursula K LeGuin

Contents

INTRODUCTION

At a glance, most days of the average human being are rather unremarkable. As the sun starts to think about showing up for the day at my house, we put the coffee on and eat breakfast. Everyone scrambles to get dressed, and then we're off and running toward whatever is on the agenda. Work, school, errands. Dishes need to be done, the cat box needs cleaning, someone has a dentist appointment. The mundane to-do lists of a home or office weekday hang out in the corner, quietly demanding attention. Unremarkable.

Yet at second glance, on a seemingly ordinary day, somewhere in the world the snow sparkles just so in the sun. Fog softens a rough edge. A newborn cries. An elder starts to fade. An old oak tree falls to the ground to see what it's like to practice resurrection in the form of decay and rebirth. Minutes pass, days are lived, months stack themselves up. Every year that ticks by reminds me how much being alive changes with the passing of time and how an understanding of time shifts with age. *The days are long, but the years are short.* Maybe this cliché is true. Maybe we just learn to see another layer of experience when caring for others, or when we are being cared for. Maybe *how* we walk through time shifts with every step we take further into our arc of life. I don't know. What I do know is that an unremarkable day can be full of wonder if we pay attention. Witnessing part of another life taking shape shapes us. Any day has the potential to serve as a poignant reminder that being alive and in community with other living things is anything but unremarkable. Any day has the potential to remind us that something like God might just be in our midst, despite everything.

Life is happening all around us, starting and stopping and starting again in ways we don't always understand. Every day we have a chance to celebrate the fact that we are on the planet at this exact moment in time. We are here, now, sharing space with other beings, some who we adore and some who we do not, some who we see clearly and some who need to be seen much more than they are. We have the opportunity to truly see them and to truly see ourselves. We can choose to view the passing of minutes, days, and years as gifts instead of something to resign ourselves to or dread. We have the opportunity to see astonishments in the mundane and blessings in the ordinary.

This book is part unsolicited advice, part musing, part blessing—but most of all it's a call to show up to life in the way that works best for you. You get to decide what to do with the words on the pages that follow. Yet wherever these words land, (and I'm guessing it'll be somewhere between the unremarkable and the astonishingly beautiful or heartbreaking) it's possible to find renewal in the ordinary dance of living.

What if you found yourself among wildflowers, walking next to whatever version of God speaks to you, slouching toward radiance? Embrace fully the ordinary dance of living. You never know what might happen.

The sun's coming up, so let's begin.

Dawn

Reflections & Ruminations

UNCHARTED

Beginnings don't always look
like we think they should,
but there is healing
in knowing
each moment is,
in fact, a new beginning.

RECLAMATION

What if you dropped
into your life
like rain drops
to a thirsty earth—
a return of life force
awakening
refreshment
the arrival of just enough abundance
to permeate your pores,
claiming you as an unfolding map
claiming you as one of the wild
claiming you as yourself?

JOY SITS QUIETLY

The other day I was talking
to a neighbor, and we decided
joy must look different than it used to.

Not that joy has ever looked the same to everyone.

But these days joy seems to find itself snuggled up
close to uncertainty, or sprouting in little spider web
cracks of the old ceramic pots that got left outside all winter.

These days joy can be kind of subtle, can't it?
There are these fleeting moments when
you can't believe how wonderful it is to be alive,

right there next to times that stand still, times
laced with worry, lament, or self-loathing—
feelings that have rather strong staying power.

And instead of telling you not to feel those things,
or offering empty reassurance that everything will be fine,
 joy just sits quietly
in your shadow
        until you notice
                she's not giving up on you.

A COMPLICATED JOY

What a complicated joy it is,

to witness light spilling into a new day

when the blood shed yesterday

is not yet dry.

What a complicated joy it is,

to absorb warm sun on your face

when the rest of you

feels numb with grief.

What a complicated joy it is,

to notice a butterfly's delicate beauty

keeping company with overripe fruit

entering a season of decay.

What a complicated joy it is,

to be wholly alive

on this hurting earth,

each day a new union of sunlight and shadow.

DAYTIME STARS

Some days
all I want to do
is sit in a sunbeam
and give the chaos of life
a respite from thriving.

Some days
what I need to do
is idle in moments
that are outside
the bounds of time.

Some days
what is best to do
is listen to songs
sung by the wild silence
of daytime stars.

7

EVERYTHING IS PRACTICE

When the hour
casts a fiery reflection
on frozen waters,
you'll know it's time
to practice wisdom
like you practice breathing—
One moment, then another
until the rhythm matches your heartbeat.
One choice, one breath, one beat
at a time.

ELEGANCE

When you can see simple truths
melting tracks through old snow,
the path taken
leads toward a sort of elegance,
the kind nature
knows so well,
the kind that leads deep
into the heart of all good things.

SECRET SPRING AS TOLD BY FERNS

There's magic in the unfurling,
in the elegance that steps
out of spring,

in growth that knows right limits
are like a secret skin, one that
keeps the earth turning,

one that keeps
the earth
turning.

HOLDING MEMORY

There in a half-forgotten woodland

Skunk Cabbage feels its way toward dawn,

Hepatica offers purple blooms to the forest

floor's monotone brown, Bloodroot dots

earth with delicate bright spots of spring hope,

a persistent promise of possibility

that all is not lost, that new life rises

even during times of grief,

that uncertainty can keep company

with cycles older than memory,

that a half-forgotten woodland

holds memory for us when

it gets too heavy to carry

so we can pick it up

again when we

are ready.

CHASING HAPPINESS

There's this thing that happens,
(maybe you know it)
when you put contentment
under condition:

When "I'll be happy as soon as"
shows up regularly
in the ongoing conversation
you have with yourself.

It feels a little like chasing something
that's just out of reach,
that's just far enough ahead
to keep you running.

CHASING HAPPINESS, PART TWO

What if happiness
isn't on the mountaintop,
at the end of the rainbow,
or around the next corner?

What if happiness
is in between gasps of air
on the mountain trail
even if you don't make it to the top?

What if happiness
is the calm inside the storm
even when dark skies
never let up?

What if happiness
is leaning into uncertainty
of the mythic unknown,
even dark corners places to find joy?

What if happiness
isn't what you've been chasing?
What if that thing you want so much
has been chasing you?

ONE SORT OF PATIENCE

Waiting for sunrise
on a spring morning
means spending time
with the sort of patience
that knows how to speak
through a chorus of waking birds,
tawny light on calm water,
elegant stems topped by subtle blush
saying, *Hello, I'm here*—
the kind of peace that
shows up when you do.

COLLECTIVE EFFERVESCENCE

Wind tumbles over rocky ledges
colliding with celestial harmonies,

a murmuration of wings, air, and light
suddenly splashing the sky

as thought and action collaborate
in a great cloud of collective effervescence.

FORSYTHIA BLOOMING

The way light spreads fingers
around a new blossom
invites wonder at what happens

when radiance shining bright,
strength uncurling after a long rest,
and the gentle energy of vulnerable things

decide to work together,
painting the earth
with everyday miracles.

WILD VOCATION

The day the lake opened up,
        bald eagles came to call

perched and preening
        high in the basswood trees,

eyes tuned to activity far below,
        while seagulls bobbed

on newly rippling water.
        Beavers headed straight to work,

chomping reeds and slapping tails,
        the sort of purposeful joy

that rises from doing
        what you are made to do.

WILDFLOWER DREAMING

We don't know
when we'll find them, but
we're going in search of flowers,

indigo, burnt umber, sky blue
pale gold, tangerine
crimson

wild ones who speak

through dreams
beneath currents
over static

delicate petals waiting

to be noticed,
a parched throat
yearning for water.

THAT GOOD NIGHT

Some seasons of life
remind us to let nature take its course

while being fully present
to what that might mean.

So let's go gentle into that good night
welcoming with open arms
the coming of the light.

Which can mean
a lot of things
if we get creative.

BEYOND QUANTIFICATION

Numbers can't paint morning
magenta, tangerine accents
whispering secrets of dawn

can't capture loon's haunting
call, echoing through
dusky evening mist

can't portray time
spent outside modern understanding,
singing ancient songs of light.

COMING OUT

The day hidden
essential things
come out
in all their splendor
is a glorious
(and courageous)
day indeed.

WHAT I LEARNED FROM MARY OLIVER

Poetry is most powerful
when no dictionary is necessary;

when anyone can find themselves
walking through words into wonder,

when meaning is a bell of simplicity
clearly ringing in truth.

THE GOOD WORK OF LIVING

When you do
the good work of living,
it's enough.
It is. Because when
you do the good work of living—
when you live and work
in ways that fill you up, even when
things are challenging, or life seems
to be conspiring against you, or systems
that need changing seem they
will forever remain unchanged;
when you live and work from
a foundation of compassion
for self and others,
when you accept your own limitations
and the limitations of your neighbors,
when you look failure in the eyes
and see it not as a deep well of despair
but a chance to pivot and
add another layer of resiliency,
when you can stay curious
yet fierce, when you can look
through the lens of the other—
when you do
the good work of living,
it's enough.

WHAT I'VE LEARNED FROM LISTENING

Silence has a lot to say.

Pine trees and wind have perfected
the urgent whispered dialogue.

Rushing water makes everything
stop and pay attention.

Winter and summer woods speak
the same language with different accents.

Words not spoken wield more power
than we think.

Intentional words whispered softly
have more value

than thoughtless words shouted
from rooftops.

ONE WORLD TURNING

There are voices in stones
harmonies traded by branch and breeze
haunting melodies sung by birds.

There is pain under anger
old wounds crying for healing
a keening echoing in the valley.

There is solace in stories—
words spoken or heard stitching deep gashes,
welcoming grief as a partner in living.

Clouds wonder, falling water
asks for witness and sun responds,
a love that keeps the world turning,

a love

       that keeps
       the world turning.

THE ART OF WALKING IN THE WOODS

If you stay outside
long enough,

meandering
slow enough,

Sure
enough

you find rainbows
on the forest floor.

ON THE BRINK

Splashes hitting rock ring out
before falling water becomes visible, that heady scent
of just thawed soil permeating air
as sunlight filters through naked branches.

Spring's muted palette expresses artistry
in exposed sandstone, last year's oak leaves,
bright green moss. Wild energy sinks
deep into your pores,

earth's transition sitting beside you
like a friend who knows how to listen.
Around the last bend, delicate cascades
of spring melt tumble down old paths,

regeneration's dance at the edge of things.
Water gushes, air claims a body, and
you sense you are on the brink,
perhaps the brink of everything.

CRASHING SILENCE

Seagull stands, regal
at the edge of a craggy cliff,
gaze pointed toward endless
horizons, deep blue water for miles.

What does this winged creature contemplate?
Not little red hearts of urgency,
all the stuff that might be coming next.
Imagine having that empty clarity.

To be still
until it's time to move,
always curious, holding
a willingness for attention

to silence inside crashing waves,
to the voice of rock and water,
to this moment, and this one
        full of everything.

A CASE FOR UNCERTAINTY

What would happen
if we all got a little less
confident in our belief,
more adept at saying,
You know, I'm really not sure.

Could not having the answer
—and saying so—
be an important
step on the path
toward peace?

WHERE SKIN MEETS AIR

Life is found
in warm fires, days
with snow or sunshine,
sometimes both, memories
of humid summer nights laying
on prickly grass as lightning bugs
blink on and off, spring melt gushing,
hoarfrost softening rusty fences, tiny
pulses of light shining through cracked
pots, remembering that gratitude is one
of those things you can be good at if you
put your mind to it, remembering that it's
okay to be sad or angry or anxious even if
you are good at gratitude, accepting silence
as a worthy partner for making peace
with unfathomable things, and in
embracing the uncertainty that
comes with putting faith in
seeds and breath and
skin meeting air.

WHERE TO FIND YOUR INSPIRATION

If you wake one day
to find your inspiration
has gone missing

take your body out
into a new day
to find it

in softly falling snowflakes
fresh tracks over frozen waters
a gaze that looks all the way up

toward that which grows
where attention
flows.

INTERPRETATIONS

One spring evening
you set aside
the weight of the day
to take a walk

through brown woods
aching to be green,
grandfather Maples and adolescent Aspen
urgently unfolding

tiny buds of promise,
a promise you accept and carry
gently, an offering
to the next one who needs it

when the time is right
when the day is heavy
when the voice of the forest
interprets the best way through.

BETWEEN DANCE AND DISASTER

Maybe the world

isn't broken,

it's just longing

for a different

sort of dance

between dark

and light.

Just think how

the world might shift

if we put our energy

into loving

intentionally,

extravagantly,

unconditionally.

Turns out,

the wild light

that is

you

is

up

for

the

challenge.

High Noon

Heart Advice & Suggestions

DON'T LET THE ROBOTS GET YOU DOWN

Inspired by *Analog Sea*

There is an energy—it's
there in the ether
on the ground
running through the soil
nestling deep in the bedrock
settling with the sediment of lakes
washing downstream via small tributaries
into the massive veins of rivers
that feed the earth's seas.

An energy untamed
by technology
refusing to be styled
into the next profitable product,
a fringe
refusing to be unraveled
by life online,
an analog sea
counterbalancing the digital fray.

HOW TO SATISFY ONE KIND OF HUNGER

Sip tea—hot tea
on a cold porch, contrast
waking you up in new ways.

Move slow enough
to pay attention—real attention
to the curve of your hand holding the cup.

Let attentiveness
to one thing at a time
be a beacon in the dark.

Let moments of all kinds
stand alone, stark beauty
enough to feed a hungry soul.

COMMUNICATION

Be mindful of shadows
in deep winter
because they may
have something to say
in a language you used to know.

UNDER THE SURFACE

See lightsomeness
in silent reflections, always
sinking deeply into a sort of peace
that might just wake the world up.

WAKING UP IN WINTER

Turn off the news.

Walk to the front door.

Notice how the doorknob feels,

cold and smooth against your bare skin.

Step outside. Pause. Eyes shut.

Wait just a moment more. Now.

Open your eyes. Look with your whole body.

Drink the vastness this space beyond holds,

revel in the wildness of the winter sky,

listen to trees cloaked in frosty glory—

a story older than others shared this day,

a story true, no matter who pays it mind,

a story worth waking up for,

even—especially—

in winter.

PRAISE THINGS THAT CANNOT LAST

Like a newborn's first gasp

Like hoarfrost at daybreak

Like the first sip of coffee on a cold morning

Like sun shining through fog

Like a perfectly ripe berry

Like muskrats swimming under ice

Like beating wings overhead

Like the blue light of dusk

Like the space between dreams and waking

Like breath at the close of life

Like a chance to say goodbye

Like this moment,

       and   this   one.

FLEETING

Observe the last winter shadow
dance across the lake,
wind at his back.

MARCH MOSS

Emulate moss
as it reaches toward
a strengthening star,
always letting its gaze
seek the light.

OUTLIERS DELIGHT

Be the one
who makes a joyful noise
when snow falls
in April
just to see
what happens.

BE LIKE A FERN

Uncurl.
Stretch toward sunlight,
thrive even in shadows.

HOW TO DISAPPEAR

Put your phone down.
Step outside, and stride toward
the center of the nearest woodland.
When you arrive deep in its wild heart,
tune your ears to the ballad sung
by branch and breeze. Notice
what you hear between notes.
Feel the pulse of moss's dialogue
with fallen leaves as an interpretation
of spring crawls up your legs like a
reborn vine, slowly weaving you
into a melody only found by
stepping away from your
digital persona toward
the texture of being
that allows you
to reclaim your
humanity.

AT WATER'S EDGE

Let the birds show you
what it's like to swoop
and dive-bomb through life

like right now is all that matters,
like right now contains enough joy

for living, wind on wings true
and strong, vision clear, song
one of everyday exuberance,

another ordinary sacred dance
that helps keep the world turning.

RESPITE

Set down your
to-do list and
pick up a bit of
wonder instead.

PROTEST & PROCLAMATION

See grace in the sun rising, new light
shining through dawn, rays casting
promise of the next right thing on morning ground.

See grace in pole beans climbing
higher each day, tendrils reaching toward
what isn't yet, but will be, someday.

See grace in thunderheads looming,
great clouds of storms yet to come,
disruptions necessary for restoration.

See grace in protest and proclamation,
rising waves of justice and peace,
humanity remembering its roots.

See grace in the setting sun, quiet nights
of replenishment, rest gently gathering
strength for another day.

PLANT WISDOM

Take your cue from a
September sunflower—
you don't always
have to be blooming.

EASIER SAID THAN DONE

Have you ever carried tension
around like a security blanket?

(Yes? Me, too.)
Here's an idea for both of us.

Put down anxiety
wrapped up as a lifestyle,

pick up a box
of peace instead.

UNDAUNTED

Always seek love
when you don't know what you're looking for.

Sit still for five minutes or walk around the block
when doing 10 things at once seems like the only option.

Look to where bright sun rises
when darkness feels too heavy to carry.

Lose the madness you're holding
when you remember your wholeness.

Be undaunted in embracing your true nature
even when the path is unclear,

especially when the path takes you
toward what you never thought possible—

toward a pace of life that isn't as frantic
as you thought it would always be.

HOW TO LIVE ALPHABETICALLY

Appreciate something.

Be a good friend.

Confront a hard thing.

Decide.

Explore your backyard.

Find peace.

Go outside more than you think you should.

Help a neighbor.

Invigorate yourself.

Journey.

Knead dough.

Listen.

Make art.

Nurture a seed.

Observe nature.

Play.

Question the status quo.

Read books.

Say what you need to say.

Tinker.

Unfollow the crowd.

Volunteer.

Wander in the wild.

Xeriscape when necessary.

Yodel, just to see what it's like.

Zigzag often.

PARTNERSHIP

Take some time
to watch the moon rise
in the east
as the sun sinks
in the west,
shadows of tandem presence
searing reflections
of peaceful partnership
deep into the heart
of all wild things.

ONE WAY TO BE A POET

Reach into silence
to pull out a word,
one that settles
just so around your shoulders
like a soft scarf might do.
Or maybe one that you must excavate
like a clay pot that's been buried for centuries.
Stay still enough to notice
how it really feels
when you've claimed it.
If you find it's not for you
return it to the ether
to be gathered by another.
Repeat as often as necessary
to adorn the world
with what only you can offer.

TRIBUTARIES

Spend enough time
in small streams
to ensure you develop
the grit and tenacity necessary
for navigating mainstream currents
without losing your sense of self.

DRINK FROM THE WISDOM WELL

Be remade with the passing of moments
as your understanding of eternity
shifts with age. Learn to see each experience

as another brushstroke of texture on
your arc of life, painting its way across time.
Let yourself drink from the wisdom well

that appears when you see unremarkable,
ordinary days as deep pools of wonder.
Notice life happening all around,

starting and stopping and starting again
in ways you may never understand.
Celebrate the confluence of creature,

plant, atmosphere, and earth
as minutes, days, and years
carve gifts of depth into a lifetime.

PRACTICE WISDOM

Give silence
enough room to expand
so those old temptresses of
growth, productivity, and worthiness

don't run away
with your peace.
Seek out practice wisdom
in all its messy,

uncomfortable nuances.
Sometimes voices in old,
tired stories need to fade
so new chapters have room to bloom.

SECRETS

Keep the kind of secrets

only trees know the way toward,
only silence has the power to unlock,
only ancient mossy boulders
        have patience to wait for,

a kind of deep magic, felt inside
warm breezes at dawn, laced
with the scent of just opened lilac blossoms
settling on your shoulders

waiting for just the right moment,

one that might unlock
a sacred mystery.

SEHNSUCHT

yearning; wistful longing.

Let summer
remind you to
slow down just enough
to feel sun-warmed skin,
juice of a tree-ripened peach
dripping down your chin, humid air
inviting hair to curl into a wild mess,
a sense of floating through days
that seem to lengthen and shorten
at the same time, a fusion of all
things melting together, making
you long for what you already have,
making you ache for moments
that stop time
just long enough
to be where
you are
now.

FAITH

Believe in the gathering
of bone and butterfly,
the reassurance of a
joyful hallelujah,
the sacred life of stones.

Believe in the peaceful
offering of river to land,
water freely given
intent on following
a timeless path.

Believe in the power
of deep listening, healing
found in a shared meal,
a kind word boldly
spoken aloud.

Believe in things
that invite aliveness,
question what takes it away,
allowing what needs to fade
to do so with grace.

MOON SHADOW

Take note of how moonlight
wakes you up in a new way,
one that keeps you inspired
one that makes you ready.

Notice how moonlight
carries what makes you weary
just far enough to allow night's
light to bathe you in holy shadow.

ON LOVE

Be reminded that
pebbles, raindrops, moss,
grassy meadows, old log cabins,
sidewalks that act as homes, foamy
lattes at your favorite cafe, a wave
to your neighbor each morning
on the way to work, robins, feral cats, orange dahlias
blooming, feedlot cattle, a lone American Bison
standing watch near a crumbling farmhouse,
red rock canyons, long-legged spiders, the person
next to you on the subway who hasn't showered
in weeks, high winds, old books, inmates
who write daily letters to small sons, children
who wake up singing, snow gently falling
on glassy water in spring—be reminded
all of this is yours to love.

A CASE FOR SLOW LIVING, IN WINTER

Take solace in cold weather
rhythms of ritual, in
ceremonies of the ordinary.
Brew tea, fold clothes, knead bread,
walk to the mailbox.
There is much to savor
in slowness, when quality
of attention allows noticing
each detail—
wisps of steam rising
soft folds in well-worn shirts
hands and dough working together
snow crunching underfoot in moonlight.
Celebrate this walk
through dark days,
this chance
to do it differently,
to revel in slowness
while light waits its turn.

A CASE FOR SLOW LIVING, IN SUMMER

Find respite in warm weather
rhythms of ritual, in ceremony
of the holy ordinary.
Pull weeds, line-dry clothes, make jam,
meander a grassy path.
There is much to be said
for lingering, when quality
of attention allows noticing
each detail—
intimacy with soil
soft flutters of well-worn shirts
hands and berries creating together
grass dewy at dawn.
Celebrate this meander
through long days,
this chance
to do it differently,
to revel in slowness
while light lingers just a bit longer.

SINGING LIFE INTO THE BONES

What if you rode a wild pony
across the desert, and saw
an old woman singing life
into brittle, dry bones?

What if you drank a glass
of deep red wine, and savored
fully a decadent meal
with no regrets?

What if you created a work
of art unapologetically, just
because you loved to paint
or write or sculpt?

What if you moved your body
just because it was made
to move, and chose rest when
idling was the best choice?

What if you approached a forest,
to be welcomed by women
who were once wolves, or wolves
who once were women?

What if you
could sing life
into your
bones?

SOLIDARITY

Stand
face to face
with bright stars
the color of the universe

Stand
shoulder to shoulder
with uncertain voices
whispering through darkness

Stand
back to back
with strength poised to
channel unwavering truth

Stand
calm, ready
to stride into the heat
of belonging here, now.

ALLEVIATION

Do what you are truly
here to do. Give in
to the pressure you feel,
because what if it's an invitation
to start? What if,
by exploring color
    by mixing ingredients
        by combining words just so
by wandering through a hardwood forest
on a quest toward inspiration,
you stumble upon the very thing
that relieves the pressure?
And what if that pressure
is replaced by joy?

Mid Afternoon

Storms & Surrender

ENOUGH

What you do for money
can't tell me
who you are, just like

who you are
can't be limited
by how you see yourself.

Your worth
can't be measured
in productivity, growth, or clouded self-perception.

No.

What interests me

is how love catches your attention,
what languages of beauty you speak
how your soul touches the earth.

You are valuable beyond measure,
a light in the world, a gift
that doesn't require a label.

ONE HARD TRUTH

If striving for perfection
brings more misery
than joy, perhaps
what you are going for
isn't so perfect after all.

I'VE NEVER MET A PERFECT PERSON (HAVE YOU?)

What if perfection
is the greatest
myth of modern times?
I mean, who decided
what 'perfect' is, anyway?
Why give that definition
so much power
when instead
you could be giving energy
to that which lights you up,
to that which softens destruction
with healing, to that which radiates
unconditional love for self, others, and the world—
a love known for casting
shadows of beauty
only created by imperfection?

HARD FEELINGS

They're like storm clouds
coming and going, waves
washing over you, wind
messing up your hair, rain
soaking to the bone.

It may seem like what you don't want
will swallow you whole, but even
the hardest feelings dissipate
when your heart is alive.

Just when they seem carved
in stone, ready to knock you over
or wreck everything that's good,
a fine mist surprises you
with its power to heal.

ASSURANCE

Some days
you feel cracked open,
conquered in the worst way
yet somehow still breathing—

air going in
and out
in
and out

finding the cracks,
seeping through them,
allowing them to be there,
acknowledging defeat.

Yet there's a light
in the distance, a beacon
even a cracked open thing
can make it to.

UNEXPECTED DELIVERIES

When the unexpected
gets dropped at your doorstep,
may you honor the enormity

of what that means
while allowing the anxiety
or fear or pain or grief

that comes with it
to sit next to whatever
solace means to you right now.

Let the hard things
keep company
with what's still good.

Because what if even the unexpected
comes with an opportunity
to practice peace?

WEEPING ROCK

I came upon you, early one
morning, quick walk on an old trail
before other things claimed the day's time.

Before today, I'd never noticed
your tears, but today I saw them,
streaming down your mossy cheeks, dripping

tiny rivers of silvery light on stone-strewn ground
seeping through cracks
from places unseen, somewhere deeper.

My tentative hands seek moisture,
hesitation giving way
to your wetness cooling my skin,

a sacral dampness showing me grief
can't be rushed, sadness isn't a thing
to escape. Tears, no matter their origin, must

be acknowledged,
felt,
held

by those who do the tending,
by those who hold space for underland parts of us
which may always be weeping.

THERE WILL BE MUSIC

Jack Gilbert
reminded us that
there will be music
despite everything.

Indeed, we must
admit that despite
everything, there will
still be music. Because
even when things seem too
hard and music feels far away,
it's still there, humming like a
persistent friend who
won't let you go it alone.

Listen with
whatever senses
are available to you
because the notes often
present themselves, even
through stormy weather
in unexpected ways—
and not just the
kind you can
hear.

LOVE IN A TIME OF GLOBAL PANIC

Where does love go
in time of global panic,
when business as usual
is disrupted by uncertainty
and the fear that underwrites
things that feel out of control?

Maybe some of it goes underground
or floats somewhere above the clouds—
during hard times, it feels like certain expressions
of love get packed away in a closet for later,
a day when things don't feel quite so hard,
a day when the world calms down.

But then, when you look closer, you see other
versions of love showing up—in the six feet between
you and your neighbor, in the way you leave
some extra bags of rice on the shelf, in
patience you practice when the house
feels too full of energy that is usually
directed elsewhere on a weekday.

Love in a time of global panic
is the same love it's always been
but it wants to show up

in new ways
through all,
for all,
adaptable,
and unceasing.

THROUGH EVERY STORM

The God I know
doesn't ban love from church
when some people don't agree
with how love presents itself.

The God I know
doesn't underwrite decisions
that claim some lifestyles
are more holy than others.

The God I know
doesn't strengthen rules
that exclude and shame
in the name of praise.

The God I know
doesn't inspire interpretations
of the Word that say, "you're wrong."
You love who you love, and that's beautiful.

The God I know
opens hearts
minds
doors
to unify all people
through every storm,
no matter who you love.

ON TRAUMA AND MIRACLE

The God I know
adds love to spaces between
everywhere across the globe.

The God I know
sits with kids who need school to feel safe/fed/heard &
parents & teachers doing the best they can with the tools they have.

The God I know
walks next to the unhoused,
those ordered to shelter in a place they didn't have.

The God I know
heals through the hands of many
offering peace when war seems to be waged from within.

The God I know
cradles the sick and those who love them
with a story that promises death isn't the end.

The God I know
fills a newly quiet earth
with birdsong and clear skies at dawn.

The God I know
is the truth of trauma & miracle
existing side by side.

EVEN WHILE GASPING

The God I know
is still on the mountain, Rizpah
seeking justice for her boys.

The God I know
is a Black man face down on pavement
gasping for breath at the hands of police.

The God I know
is more outraged by white supremacy's violence
than church doors ordered shut.

The God I know
is a white person
confronting her own racist ideals.

The God I know
is calling us all in
to do the anti-racist work

of rebuilding the kingdom
one truth at a time until
all lives really do matter.

SWIMMING THROUGH INTENTIONS

Do you ever feel lost
in a sea of good intentions? The kind
that get continually swept out to sea
by waves of doubt or societal pressure or
unconscious bias, the kind that seem to build
and get more powerful
if you take your eyes away
for even a second?

It can feel hard to do the right thing,
to know what the right thing to do is.

But maybe not knowing is another invitation to start,
to not let a rough, unfamiliar sea stop you
from doing whatever it is you set out to do.

What if, instead, you use discomfort as a catalyst
to do something that contributes to the healing
of the world? Something that adds
the kind of power that the world truly needs?

At the end of the day, there's no right answer
on what that something is. There is only
the next right action to take toward
that elusive, more beautiful world.

CONSIDERING THE WORLD

Can it be mended by tears, healed
through scars, grow new skin
where disease still ravages the old?
Can you and I, them, us—can we
walk together on shattered ground
taking the pieces that lay glowing
and pile them up to use the breath
of life to ignite a new fire, one hot
enough to forge a way forward?
One where Rage, Guilt, Grief, and Shame
somehow come together, reaching
across the wall of lived experience
with compassion and love to build
a system that rises like a wave
powerful enough
to wash hate and
power-over
away?

RELEASE

There are days
when boxing up
unneeded things

(from old shoes to
unsolicited advice to
dark thoughts to
toxic positivity)

is like exhaling
a breath you didn't
know you were holding.

THAW

Do you feel it, way out
on the arctic horizon?
A tiny beam of light shining, just now
reaching the frozen bits, softening
the parts nestled deep
in the ice, an act of survival
that held life for you
when it was too much
to carry, when it was clear
growth wasn't the way forward,
the kind of light only found
after burrowing deep and waiting
for the right moment
to emerge.

BELONGING

If you can only
be sure of one thing,

be sure of how your presence
here on earth is essential.

Nothing would be the same
if your thread wasn't woven

deep into this great tapestry,
woven over millennia

by the synergies that make life possible
on this fair planet—

earth, fire, water, air
meet in space and across time

to tell the story
of your worth—

that you matter, and that's the part
of the story to focus on.

Hard days will still be hard:
but you are woven deep

into something bigger
than yourself,

something that wouldn't exist
if your thread wasn't here,

something that always remains
true even if those hard days stack up.

The world may be
an uncertain place

but your place
in it isn't.

You matter.
Your place is here.

LAYING IT DOWN

One autumn,
you started to surrender
to cooling conditions,
age slowing you into softening;
reflection;
blooming of another kind.

One autumn,
you displayed the reminder
that the aged leaf is one
telling the story
of life lived
to the fullest.

One autumn,
you showed us wisdom
is a different sort of beauty,
one requiring letting go
of the constant quest
for advancement.

One autumn,
you demonstrated
decline can mean
laying down growth to
take up elder-hood
in its place.

SURRENDER

Sunflowers follow
their namesake's every move,
even when doing so means delicate
necks are bathed in shadow,

and garden pests, the ones
eating holes in the bean leaves,
hum with growing satisfaction,
tiny translucent beings

circling round and round and round
again

tiny bodies eventually falling
one by one to the ground

until each sunflower lowers
its gaze for good, neck exposed,

letting go, dropping

into the sweet darkness
of a new season.

Did you really think
they could grow forever?

WHAT KALE WILL SHOW YOU
IF YOU PAY ATTENTION

One day as you walk
through unkempt rows
around robust weeds
past that which has been nibbled
by resident wild things,
you find you want to lament
all you haven't done
all that has been lost
all that may never be.
But you cannot, you see.
Because the kale has grown
into a forest of abundance,
one that won't stand for
self-loathing or bemoaning
all the work still to come.
The kale is quick to remind
you of all that flourishes
despite persistent worry
that you're never
quite enough.

RHAPSODY IN ORANGE

The storm rolled in,
all black thundery clouds,
winds that only the great
plains know how to howl.

Hatches battened down,
the people turned inward
while the storm blew itself out
with a hazy orange glow,

splicing open the heavens
as a spectrum of color dipped
to earth, a message from wherever
rainbows get their voices

telling us to consider
leaving one eye slightly open
always on the lookout
for unexpected rapture.

THE WILDEST KIND OF LOVE

Maybe you're lost
far from home
unsure if home even exists
afraid that home is no longer there.

Many are disoriented.
Routes are long and hard.
Uncertainty abounds.
What felt stable and safe can vanish

in a blink of an eye
as a stiff wind gusts from the west
in a year that is already
beating you down.

Sorrow and fear are real
in a year like this.
Anxiety and anger are real
in a year like this.

It's normal to long to return
to what feels like home
especially when what you knew as home
might not be where you left it.

It's not easy to remember home
is with you always—a wildness
etched in your bones,
coursing through your veins,

an ancient agreement of shadow and light
a raw embodiment of love
capable of weathering
any firestorm.

But it is.
Even in a year like this.

A BOAT CALLED CLARITY

We're all in some kind of storm.
But not the same boat.
Some of us don't even have a boat.

Some of us are really smart, even wise.
But no one knows the right answer.
There's no *one solution fits all.*

Can there be an "all clear" siren
when not much was clear
before the storm hit?

We don't all know the same version of God.
But there are collective "gods" of our time,
gods that need to be wrestled with.

What if we learned something
that could only be illuminated
by stormy weather?

WHEN WORDS FAIL

Sometimes when you are trying
to come up with just the right words,
a description of some astonishing

>   or joyful
>   or heartbreaking thing,
sun breaks through clouds

like a child peeking through filmy curtains
or a gentle breeze lifts hair that fell
across tired eyes

or an urban fox holds your gaze,
a streak of wildness refusing to be tamed.
Sometimes words aren't enough

because experiencing life in full
requires learning a language
that can only be felt.

FIREWEED AND FURY

The twenty-seventh time
someone describes you as gentle,
you wonder what it would take
to be described as fierce or strong or bold,
    words that conjure
             Joan of Arc
                  or Beyoncé
                        or Nadia Bolz-Weber,

women who seem to step fully into their power
without worrying about the consequences

women who surely feel fear
and do what they need to do anyway

women who stand up loudly
for what they believe is right

women who consciously
embody the space they need

women who are angry and
somehow channel rage into right action.

"You need to talk louder," they say.

"Get up there in front! Make sure to smile."

So you think, "Okay. More public speaking will help,"
or at least a robust willingness to say
"Hey, look at me. Pay attention to what I'm saying."

You wonder about all the women
        who aren't in history books
women
            who haven't sold lots of albums
women
        who haven't made *Time Magazine's*
                list of most influential people,
women
        who demonstrate what strength is
                in an ordinary life,
        what boldness looks like
                in an ordinary day,
        what it means to be fierce
                in an ordinary way.

The twenty-eighth time
someone describes you as gentle,
a quiet fury burns into clarity, ashes revealing
you can move softly through life
and still be a force,
one that has the power
to impact the world in subtle ways,
like how patience and spring sunlight
have the power to transform wildfire into blossom.

BOX OF DARKNESS

This was not the year you wanted
but it's the year you got—so what
will you do with it? Wrap it tight
in hopes of nothing seeping out,
wait for someone to collect it
on garbage day? Rage against
whatever machine has got you down?
Drown your sorrows?

That's tempting.

Rage and sorrow
can be necessary clearing tools
through thorns. Grief journeys
must be fully traveled. Truly
tending to and healing wounds
often takes far longer
than you think it should.

Yet what if you accept
what's been handed to you
as something to move through
instead of wish away? This doesn't
mean you have to like it or find meaning

in hard moments as they fall. It just means
you won't waste another ounce
of energy longing for a different past.

What you have is the present.

Box of darkness it may be, it's yours
to open and yours to see what happens
if it's simply allowed to be here—
feet in soil, face to the sky.

Golden Hour

Blessings & Invitations

MAY YOU ALWAYS

Listen to the story
in the cracked coffee mug,
in the worn-out shirt that feels
too good to throw away, in the ever-
present weeds lining the garden fence,
in old paths winding through forests,
in too-tall grass and how trees that fell
years ago encourage saplings to turn
expectant faces toward the sky while
learning what it's like to tunnel
roots deeper into the earth,
always remembering to
listen to the story.

LIGHT IN WINTER

May the brightness
of a sunny day
in winter
remind you to tap into
your invincible summer,
whatever that
might mean,
so you can joyfully
traverse any snowy
paths that may appear
in your future.

ANOTHER MAGIC KINGDOM

Take me back
to that place
under a quiet sky
where trumpeter swans
make joyful music,
fish laze beneath
two feet of ice, snow
whispers softly underfoot.
Remind me to pause
just long enough
to be swept up
by the magic
of the kingdom.

THIS I HOPE

I hope there are days
when fog makes you feel held

when fireflies dancing claim
your attention over scrolling

when you can taste clarity in drops of rain
running down your face

when you can remember to lean deeply
into that which roots you to earth

when you can remember
to look up in wonder.

CHILD OF MINE
(for Eva)

May you always know
strength
courage
joy
in whatever form your
life takes.

May you always feel
fierce
compassionate
empowered
in whatever ways your
life needs.

May you always find
peace
purpose
freedom
in whatever direction your
life moves.

May you always know
you are whole
brave
loved
beyond measure.

SLOUCHING TOWARD RADIANCE

May you allow yourself
all sorts of feelings,
even if they aren't
defined by sunbursts.
May light and dark
both find a home
in your days.
May you gift yourself
simple gestures of respect,
the kind that result in love
encouraging sparkle and shadow
to fall together toward radiance.

LIFE AS ART

May the weeks ahead
whether beautiful
or difficult
or both,
be full
of opportunities taken,
the kind that allow
getting lost
in whatever art
focuses thought
cleanses spirit
offers joy—
the kind of joy
that hands itself over,
taking the place
of those elusive
happy endings.

LIFE AS ART, PART TWO

Look at the pain,
the beauty, everything
in between.

Make something with it.

Let every experience
be another brushstroke
on your canvas of living.

LIFE AS ART, PART THREE

What if you could lose yourself
in the art of being alive?

Even when feeling adrift, unsure
what world to inhabit, what if

you kept doing simple things
that focus attention,

like slowly kneading bread
in late afternoon sun

noticing a tiny creature's footprint
on a snow-covered log in the woods

savoring the act of witnessing
tangerine and violet colliding just after dawn?

Would it help identify the world
you're supposed to inhabit?

Would it help you continue evolving
into the person you are always becoming?

Would losing yourself in the art of living
be a path toward a more beautiful world,

the one that's always there when you
remember to be astonished by it?

EMBERS OF JOY

I want to invite you

to cast aside the weighty world
    & float above worry,
        a puffy cloud on a summer day.

to feel your feet on the ground,
    rooting deeply to earth
        solid rock on a mountain's north face.

to see each moment
    as it aches to been seen, holding
        presence as effortlessly as breath.

to be here, now
    doing things that leave
        embers of joy
            slowly burning
                in their wake.

ORDINARY MAGIC

Discover your
enchanted places
and visit often enough
to reclaim your belief
in any magic that's
gone missing.

FORGING MEANING AND MATTER

Refuse the siren song
that says *"numb hard feelings"*

just because they hurt. Accept
that joys can keep company with sorrows.

Open to the uncertain wonder
of walking through a forest at dawn,

fog rising from the lake,
day stretched ahead like a canvas waiting

for the combination of paint and time
that will transform it from blank slate

to something lovingly and curiously created
from the rawness of living.

This is the fire. This is what you need
to meet and embrace

to fully meld meaning and
matter into a life fully forged.

ONE MORE NOTE ON JOY

Seize opportunities for joy.
Even if they are few
and far between
they deserve to be held.

Dusk

On Solitude & Keeping Company

COMPLIMENTARY

Most evenings
when air is heavy with heat
pair well with chilled wine

or raspberry iced tea, maybe
with a splash of sparkling water
if wine isn't for you,

a song sung by frogs
one buzzing bumblebee
just enough solitude to invite

reflections of all sorts
as dusk thinks about
making an appearance.

POSSIBLE METHODS OF ENCHANTMENT

I. A maiden wandering
through tangled vines
path unclear yet
magnetic.

II. An old woman rocking slowly
near the edge of deep woods
chair by the fire creaking
to the rhythm of her magic.

III. Swans soaring overhead
searching for water clear of ice
wings stretched out, feathers
working their wonders.

IV. You, fully emerging,
a wildly soft creature craving
a taste of what can only
be found in the search.

WORLD ON FIRE

My backyard
isn't burning, but
yours over there is
which is my call
to bear witness
to the unthinkable.

I can't know
what it's like, not really,
to be in your body
on that savanna or in those streets
seeing those images
knowing they are so close
to home,

knowing they are
your home.
Feeling the heat.
Fleeing the fires.
Freeing what you can.
Leaving what you can't.

I can't know
what it's like,
but I can be sure
not to look away.

I can be sure
to listen.
I can be sure
to act.

A global community
calls for all hands
on deck.

HIGH COUNTRY BURNING

Now it's my forest burning,
the one that holds family memories
from before I was born.

I want that land to be on the other side of the fire line.
I want the old buildings to survive.
I want the rain to stop the flames

before they ravage trees
the beetles already took
before the sky gets any darker with smoke.

Yet the fires burn, turning what was
into cinders, and through our tears
we see the outline of a mountain range,

a Mummy that can withstand any heat,
holding us against its bones
as new life promises to rise from the ash.

ON COMMUNITY

I see your humanness
and offer you mine—
together we walk
side by side,
imperfect, but together.

Sometimes there is limping
or one of us has to be carried,
but when we take turns
it works out okay
in the end.

Because along the way
there's time to celebrate
how beautiful being human can be
when we fully acknowledge
we belong to each other.

POET SOLITAIRE

You don't need permission
to write in the direct path of the wind,
wander whimsically in wild places,
seek solitude in secret sanctuaries.

You might say warmth is necessary,
and so is permission, sometimes,
but not when it comes to tapping
into the pulse that rises

from solitude
from walking the edge of discomfort
from any opening that leads
to the untamed silence of the soul.

You need community, it's true.
We all do.

You also need at least a bit
of time as a desert solitaire
riding through the night
in search of forbidden fruit.

SELF RELIANCE

Somewhere in the sea
between dreaming and wakefulness
I see the future
a point of energy
bobbing in churning waves
a far off nearby place
reached every minute and never
always arriving to find it's still up ahead—
just keep swimming,
says the dream
and I awake thinking
I will if you carry me.

THE WAY OUT

Maybe it seems like
disappointments lurk
around every other corner,

that the universe decided
to stop handing out signs,
like sorrow and rage collide daily

just to spite you
as history keeps repeating
itself, and not in ways that feel good.

If this is the case, it's fair
to feel despair—to wonder
how there could ever be a way out of this.

It's fair to feel that way.
It's not wrong, either.
It's also not the end of the story.

No one can take your despair
away from you—
you know this already.

Despair is one
of those things that rage
and sorrow fight over.

So, no—no one can take your despair
away from you—but you can
look it in the eye on the clear days

and say, "Hello rage, sorrow.
Walk with me awhile.
The weather's fine."

The weather's fine, and
even when it turns we'll continue
walking together until we're through.

AT THE EDGE OF THE WOODS

Won't you keep me company
like a shy deer keeps company
with low hanging leaves

mist covering still waters
slow rain falling to earth
tender grasses swaying, extending

invitations to savor
invitations to walk lightly,
invitations to listen fully,

confident trust and attentiveness
are conspiring to fall in step
toward belonging.

YOU, ME & LOVE

There is something unbreakable
binding us to ourselves and
all other living things.

It is so strong,
even when it looks broken
it's not.

Try as we might
to go it alone or give up entirely,
we are in this together.

UNCONDITIONAL LOVE

I believe in you
even when you can't see
through your own uncertainty.

I believe in you
even though the rain
doesn't seem to be letting up.

I believe in you
even if past traumas
feel etched in your bones.

I believe in you
no matter what it takes
to clear a path forward.

I believe in you
even when you
don't.

PRAIRIE'S EDGE

Look beyond sunset
past the dusty mailbox
swinging on old hinges,
rusty squeaks fading to nothing
as the breeze dies with the light,
where there lies a field of wild daisies,
big bluestem, sideoats grama &
enough milkweed to intoxicate
monarchs for days, a place
where stillness and motion
melt together,
a fondue of peace
ready to be dipped into
by anyone lost in the dark
who is willing to look further
than usual, just past the edge,
just beyond sunset.

SIGHTLINES

Boreal forests
at dusk
hold stories
of mystery deep
in wild murmurs
masquerading
as fallen leaves
and in the way a path
changes as you learn
to see in the dark.

LAST ONE STANDING

Life is part trauma,
part triumph,
and a good life happens
when triumph is the last one standing,
     fiddle in hand,
         drum beating,
               voices lifted in song
at the joy of another morning.

PARTING WORDS
Blood, Bone, and Soil

TAKE A MOMENT TO CONSIDER THE CURRENT STATE OF
THINGS. Your life, at this moment, may feel joyful, full of
fantastic momentum, days drenched in delight. Or maybe
it feels like a slog through a boggy swamp swarming with relentless
mosquitoes. Maybe you are right in the middle of the hardest period
of time you've ever experienced, one marked by loss, depression, illness,
chaos, or strained relationships.

No matter what your life circumstances are, the things that have already
come to pass will always be with you. What has already happened is part
of your lived experience, and it always will be, whether the events that
transpired were worthy of celebration or a doorway to heart-wrenching
grief. You can continue striving, or look for the next area of growth, or set
your sights on what's yet to come. You can lament what has happened. You
can also simply acknowledge whatever you've navigated and set it down
gently to be absorbed into the soil of your life.

Set it down, maybe even work it into the soil a bit. (This is different from
burying it never to be seen again.) Allow it to feed whatever it is that
needs to happen next—even if what needs to happen next is completely
unknown. Even if what needs to happen next isn't something you would
have chosen.

Zora Neale Hurston said that there are some years that pose questions and some years that provide answers. For most of us, the question years far outnumber those that answer. It can be tough to discern what sort of year it's been until decades later, because some questions take an awfully long time to answer. Answers are often quite different than we want them to be. Answers sometimes come in the form of another question.

However you are feeling here on the cusp of whatever is next, know this: You are not defined by what has happened to you or what you have achieved. You are not your trauma, or even your successes. Those things have plenty of impact on your life, but they aren't the core of who you are. You are a human being full of nuance and light and shadow and pain and healing, something hard to define with spoken language. You are a part of the earth's body, part of the human collective, part of a mystical universe experiencing life on a planet of blood and bone and soil.

Look at what has come to pass, see it through the lens of curiosity, and set it down gently. Allow whatever parts of it you can to provide nourishment. Identify what's within your control, and acknowledge what's not. Use the strengths that you have, in the aspects of your life where you have agency, to cultivate the conditions you most need in order to thrive, and to help others to do the same. Let the blood, bone, and soil of your human life provide a foundation for your spirit as you keep on slouching toward a radiant sky.

We're in this thing together, this day and always.

ACKNOWLEDGMENTS

A collection of poems always feels like a living, breathing thing to me, and I think it's because the words that come together do so because of relationships. And no matter how those relationships evolve (whether they are with other humans or with the natural world), they add layers and texture to the experience of living. Many thanks to Juliana Aragón Fatula and the late Burt Bradley for giving me valuable feedback on some poems that made it into this collection. Thanks to Leslie M. Browning and the community of writers at Homebound Publications for providing a home for these words and fellowship along the way. Thanks to Emily Anderson for partnership in pairing poetry and paintings—your vibrant images make the words come even more to life. And as always, thank you to my family, especially Nick and Eva, for continuing to walk alongside me day in and day out.

END NOTES

Analog Sea, the inspiration behind the poem titled "Don't Let the Robots Get You Down," is an offline publisher of printed books. You can ask them to add you to their mailing list by writing them a letter. Visit analogsea. com for their mailing address.

I first heard the story of Rizpah on the mountain (as referenced in "Even While Gasping") in a live sermon by Austin Channing Brown.

"There Will Be Music" was inspired by Jack Gilbert's poem "A Brief for the Defense" as found in his collection *Refusing Heaven.* [Knopf; Reprint edition (March 13, 2007)]

"Prairie's Edge" was first published in *South Dakota in Poems,* an anthology curated and edited by Christine Stewart-Nuñez, published by the South Dakota Poetry Society in 2020.

ABOUT THE ARTIST

Emily Anderson paints brightly colored impressionist landscapes depicting the precious and protected lands of North America in hopes of spreading joy and appreciation for the beauty around us. She happily lives in the woods of Marine on St. Croix, Minnesota with her loving family. Learn more about her work at emilyandersonartwork.com.

ABOUT THE AUTHOR

Heidi Barr is the author of *12 Tiny Things, Woodland Manitou, Cold Spring Hallelujah, What Comes Next,* and *Prairie Grown,* as well as the editor of *The Mindful Kitchen.* She works as a wellness coach and occasionally coordinates with yoga teachers and organic farms to offer retreat experiences.

A commitment to cultivating ways of being that are life-giving and sustainable for people, communities and the planet provides the foundation for her work.

Heidi studied Health and Wellness at Luther College and has a Master of Arts degree from Luther Seminary in Faith and Health Ministries. She lives in Minnesota with her family where they tend a large vegetable garden, explore nature and do their best to live simply. Learn more at heidibarr.com.

HOMEBOUND
PUBLICATIONS

We are an award-winning independent publisher founded in 2011 striving to ensure that the mainstream is not the only stream. More than a company, we are a community of writers and readers exploring the larger questions we face as a global village. It is our intention to preserve contemplative storytelling. We publish full-length introspective works of creative non-fiction, literary fiction, and poetry.

WWW.HOMEBOUNDPUBLICATIONS.COM

CPSIA information can be obtained
at www.ICGtesting.com
Printed in the USA
JSHW020719260122
22286JS00004B/4

9 781953 340504